30

Days

with

Wesley

a prayer book

Richard Buckner, Editor

BEACON HILL PRESS
OF KANSAS CITY

Copyright 2012
by Beacon Hill Press of Kansas City

ISBN 978-0-8341-2833-0

Printed in China

Cover Design: Arthur Cherry
Internal Design: Sharon Page

Library of Congress Cataloging-in-Publication

30 days with Wesley : a prayer book / Richard Buckner, editor.
    p. cm.
    Includes bibliographical references.
    ISBN 978-0-8341-2833-0 (flex cover)
    1. Spiritual life—Methodist Church. 2. Methodist Church—Prayers and devotions. 3. Devotional literature. 4. Wesley, John, 1703-1791. 5. Wesley, Charles, 1707-1788. I. Buckner, Richard, 1961- II. Wesley, Charles, 1707-1788. III. Wesley, John, 1703-1791.
    BX8349.S68A15 2012
    242'.8—dc23

                                                                                                2011051707

10 9 8 7 6 5 4 3 2 1

Contents

The Lord's Prayer*

Our Father in heaven,
hallowed be your Name,
your kingdom come,
your will be done,
on earth as in heaven.
Give us today our daily bread.
Forgive us our sins
as we forgive those
who sin against us.
Save us from the time of trial,
and deliver us from evil.
For the kingdom, the power,
and the glory are yours,
now and forever. Amen.

*BCP

Introduction

Christians pray in different ways. Many emphasize spontaneous prayers in their devotional lives, preferring to express themselves freely in their own words. Others prefer to pray scriptures, especially the Psalms, and traditional prayers from prayer books, enjoying the guidance and insight that comes from others who have walked with God in the past. Both ways are wonderful means of grace that can open a person's heart to God's transforming and healing presence, and both ways can work hand-in-hand in the lives of God's people. This prayer book, while giving much attention to using the Scriptures and written prayers as vehicles for a deeper communion with God, is designed to include and enhance a person's own freely expressed personal prayers.

There are different kinds of prayer books. Most prayer books include space for personal prayers, but many prayer books encompass the personal part and go beyond it. Although some prayer books are designed for people to use alone, the most widely used books are for communities. Since a prayer book contains the prayers to pray and the scriptures to read for different hours of the day, the members of an entire community can join in prayer at the same time without being in the same place. These kinds of books gather all the personal voices of a community together into one common voice of prayer to God.

30 Days with Wesley can be used for either personal or community-wide prayer. Each of the thirty days is divided into morning and evening prayer times. Following the design of traditional Christian prayer, each morning-prayer section includes an opening psalm, a hymn, two additional psalm passages with accompanying prayers, an optional Scripture reading, an extended prayer with space for personal prayers, space for the Lord's Prayer, and a dismissal prayer. The evening-prayer section is a shorter version of the morning section and is prefaced with self-examination questions to encourage spiritual growth. Evening prayer concludes with space for writing personal reflections or meditations.

Most of the prayers and self-examination questions are based on the prayers of John Wesley. This eighteenth-century Anglican priest and founder of Methodism composed three sets of weekly prayers: "Forms of Prayer," designed for individuals; "Prayers for Families"; and "Prayers for Children." As a priest in the Church of England, Wesley was well acquainted with the prayer book of his community, *The Book of Common Prayer*. For Wesley praying was a special means of grace, and this understanding is reflected in his written prayers. The prayers in this book have in most cases been adapted from Wesley's work, using more contemporary language, plural pronouns to emphasize community, and rearranged structure to reflect traditional Christian prayer patterns. This last adaptation is found especially in the extended morning prayers, or intercessions. The intercessions are Wesley's words rearranged to include repeated lines of praise or supplication between the different prayer petitions.

Almost all the hymn lyrics are adapted from the work of Charles Wesley, John's brother. In a couple of cases (days 15 and 16) the lyrics are translations by John from the compositions of German composers.

The prayers in this book are not intended to replace impromptu personal prayers. As mentioned earlier, the prayers are in many ways enhancements to the prayer life; they are like signposts guiding the worshipper into more thoughtful experiences with God. The hope is that they will lead a person to greater depths of expression in his or her personal prayers. Inviting others to pray at the same times each day, either in person or while separated by distance, can transform these prayers into a community event. Knowing others are praying the same prayers at the same times each day reinforces the bond of love and mission Christians share as members of Christ's body.

The hymn lyrics, psalms, and other Scripture readings, along with Wesley's prayers, should all be read or spoken as a two-way conversation with God. Worshippers should meditate on the words, listening for God's voice, and then allow the same words combined with their personal prayers to carry their responses back to God. As each day passes, people may record their thoughts, spiritual progress, and insights in the meditation spaces following evening prayers. This will leave a journal of the personal and communal experiences of these thirty days for later review and reflection.

Praying at set times of the day is a practice that predates the time of Christ. It is rooted in Israel's daily Temple sacrifices (see Exod. 29:38-39), transformed by synagogues into sacrifices of praise during times of exile (see Ps. 119:164), enhanced by the rhythmic and disciplined prayer times of Christian monks, and developed by different Christian communities into prayer books used by clergy and laity alike. With the help of the Holy Spirit, the hours of prayer can be a means through which time is sanctified (set apart for God), communities are united, hearts are edified, and God's transforming love is experienced.

Though this book is only a brief introduction to the richness found in the many prayer books belonging to the body of Christ, it is hoped that it will open up new vistas in the prayer lives of those who pray from it and be a pathway to deeper encounters with God. May the blessing of Almighty God, the Father, the Son, and the Holy Spirit, be upon all who use it. Amen.

DAY 1 † Morning Prayer

> O Lord, open my lips, and my mouth will declare your praise (Ps. 51:15).

Psalm 100:1-2

Shout for joy to the LORD, all the earth.
Worship the LORD with gladness;
come before him with joyful songs.

Glory to the Father, and to the Son, and to the Holy Spirit: as it was in the beginning, is now, and will be forever. Amen.

Hymn

O for a thousand tongues to sing
My great Redeemer's praise,
The Glories of my God and King,
The triumphs of His grace!

Psalm 63:1-3

O God, you are my God,
earnestly I seek you;
my soul thirsts for you,
my body longs for you,
in a dry and weary land
where there is no water.

I have seen you in the sanctuary
and beheld your power and your glory.
Because your love is better than life,
my lips will glorify you.

Prayer

O Lord, make it our delight to praise you, to call to mind your loving-kindness, and to offer the sacrifice of thanksgiving.

Psalm 149:1-3

Sing to the LORD a new song,
    his praise in the assembly of the saints.
Let Israel rejoice in their Maker;
    let the people of Zion be glad in their King.
Let them praise his name with dancing
    and make music to him with tambourine and harp.

Prayer

O Lord, we desire to adore your sacred name, who has in your goodness brought us in safety to behold the beginning of a new day.

Scripture Reading (Optional)   Revelation 7:9-12

Intercessions

Let us lift up our hearts in praise and thanksgiving to our Heavenly Father, praying,

Glory to you, O most adorable Father.

You are the end for which we were created, and we can expect no happiness but in you.

Glory to you, O most adorable Father.

Give your strength to your servants, that your love may fill our hearts.

Glory to you, O most adorable Father.

Let your love be the motive of all we do today with our understanding, our health, our time, and all other talents you have given us.

Glory to you, O most adorable Father.

(Offer personal prayers.)

The Lord's Prayer

Dismissal

O Father, do more and better for us than we can either desire or deserve, for the sake of our blessed Savior and Redeemer, Jesus Christ, to whom, with you and the Holy Spirit, be all praise and glory, now and forever. Amen.

DAY 1 † Evening Prayer

Self-Examination

(Reflect on the day, using the following questions as a guide, confess any departures from the law of love, and ask God for forgiveness.)

- Have I done anything that was not in some way to the glory of God?
- Have I failed to do what good I could?
- Have I unnecessarily grieved anyone by word or deed?

Opening

O God, come to my assistance; O Lord, make haste to help me (Ps. 69:2, DRA).*

Glory to the Father, and to the Son, and to the Holy Spirit: as it was in the beginning, is now, and will be forever. Amen.

Revelation 19:1-2

Hallelujah!
Salvation and glory and power belong to our God,
    for true and just are his judgments.

Intercessions

(Offer personal prayers.)

The Lord's Prayer

Dismissal

O Shepherd of Israel, graciously receive us this night and ever into your protection. We ask this through Jesus Christ our Lord. Amen

---

*Psalm 70:1 in most modern versions of the Bible.

Personal Meditations

DAY 2 † Morning Prayer

> O Lord, open my lips, and my mouth will declare your praise (Ps. 51:15).

Psalm 100:3

Know that the LORD is God.
>> It is he who made us, and we are his;
>> we are his people, the sheep of his pasture.

Glory to the Father, and to the Son, and to the Holy Spirit: as it was in the beginning, is now, and will be forever. Amen.

Hymn

Praise the Lord who reigns above
And keeps his court below
Praise the holy God of love
And all his greatness show.

Psalm 5:3

In the morning, O LORD, you hear my voice;
>> in the morning I lay my requests before you
>> and wait in expectation.

Prayer

We humble ourselves, O Lord of heaven and earth, before your glorious majesty.

Psalm 29:1-4, 10-11

Ascribe to the LORD, O mighty ones,
>> ascribe to the LORD glory and strength.
Ascribe to the LORD the glory due his name;
>> worship the LORD in the splendor of his holiness.
The voice of the LORD is over the waters;
>> the God of glory thunders,
>> the LORD thunders over the mighty waters.
The voice of the LORD is powerful;
>> The voice of the LORD is majestic.

. . . .

The Lord sits enthroned over the flood;
the Lord is enthroned as King forever.
The Lord gives strength to his people;
the Lord blesses his people with peace.

Prayer

O Lord, we acknowledge your eternal power, wisdom, goodness, and truth and render you our heartfelt thanks for all the acts of kindness you have poured upon us.

Scripture Reading (Optional)   2 Thessalonians 3:10-13

Intercessions

With hearts filled with gratitude, let us bless and adore our almighty and everlasting Father, praying,

Praise to you, O God, the Giver of all good gifts.

Blessed be your love for giving your Son to die for our sins, for the means of grace, and for the hope of glory.

Praise to you, O God, the Giver of all good gifts.

Make us every day more zealous and diligent to use every opportunity to build up our souls in your faith, love, and obedience.

Praise to you, O God, the Giver of all good gifts.

Make yourself always present to our minds, and let your love fill and rule our souls in all those places, associations, and activities to which you call us this day.

Praise to you, O God, the Giver of all good gifts.

(Offer personal prayers.)

The Lord's Prayer

Dismissal

O Father, grant that we, together with all our brothers and sisters in Christ, may share in a joyful resurrection, through him who lives and reigns with you and the Holy Spirit, one God, forever and ever. Amen.

DAY 2 ✝ Evening Prayer

Self-Examination

(Reflect on the day, using the following questions as a guide, confess any departures from the law of love, and ask God for forgiveness.)

- Did I think of God first and keep him in my thoughts throughout the day?
- Have I considered anything too valuable to give up to please or serve my neighbor?

Opening

O God, come to my assistance; O Lord, make haste to help me (Ps. 69:2, DRA).

Glory to the Father, and to the Son, and to the Holy Spirit: as it was in the beginning, is now, and will be forever. Amen.

Ephesians 1:3

Praise be to the God and Father of our Lord Jesus Christ, who has blessed us in the heavenly realms with every spiritual blessing in Christ.

Intercessions

(Offer personal prayers.)

The Lord's Prayer

Dismissal

Almighty God, be our guide, our hope and our help, our joy and our comfort, now and forevermore, through Jesus Christ our Redeemer. Amen.

Personal Meditations

DAY 3 † Morning Prayer

Psalm 100:4-5

Enter [the LORD's] gates with thanksgiving
and his courts with praise;
give thanks to him and praise his name.
For the LORD is good and his love endures forever;
his faithfulness continues through all generations.

Glory to the Father, and to the Son, and to the Holy Spirit: as it was in the beginning, is now, and will be forever. Amen.

Hymn

All praise to our redeeming Lord,
Who joins us by his grace
And bids us, each to each restored,
Together seek his face.

Psalm 89:5-8

The heavens praise your wonders, O LORD,
your faithfulness too, in the assembly of the holy ones.
For who in the skies above can compare with the LORD?
Who is like the LORD among the heavenly beings?
In the council of the holy ones God is greatly feared;
he is more awesome than all who surround him.
O LORD God Almighty, who is like you?
You are mighty, O LORD, and your faithfulness surrounds you.

Prayer

O most great and mighty Lord, the possessor of heaven and earth, all the angels rejoice in blessing and praising you, the Father of spirits, for you have created all things and spread your tender mercies over all your works.

Psalm 33:1-3

Sing joyfully to the LORD, you righteous;
  it is fitting for the upright to praise him.
Praise the LORD with the harp;
  make music to him on the ten-stringed lyre.
Sing to him a new song;
  play skillfully, and shout for joy.

Prayer

O Lord, we desire thankfully to acknowledge your generosity to us and your particular grace and favor to us in Jesus Christ, our merciful Redeemer.

Scripture Reading (Optional)   Romans 13:11-14

Intercessions

With humble gratitude to our eternal and merciful Father, who gives us all blessings, let us pray,

Hear us, O gracious Father.

Let us not live but to love you and to glorify your name.

Hear us, O gracious Father.

Pour into us the whole spirit of humility and fill our souls entirely with it.

Hear us, O gracious Father.

Do with us what seems best in your own eyes; only give us the mind that was in your Son, our Savior; let us learn from him to be meek and lowly.

Hear us, O gracious Father.

(Offer personal prayers.)

The Lord's Prayer

Dismissal

O Father, direct us so to pass through the things that are not eternal so that we may not lose the things that are eternal, but at last be received into your presence, where there is fullness of joy, and be seated at your right hand, where there are pleasures forevermore, through Jesus Christ our Savior. Amen.

DAY 3 † Evening Prayer

Self-Examination

(Reflect on the day, using the following questions as a guide, confess any departures from the law of love, and ask God for forgiveness.)

- Have I given myself credit for any good that God did by my hand?
- Have I, when I thought so, said, "I am in the wrong?"

Opening

O God, come to my assistance; O Lord, make haste to help me (Ps. 69:2, DRA).

Glory to the Father, and to the Son, and to the Holy Spirit: as it was in the beginning, is now, and will be forever. Amen.

Revelation 4:11

You are worthy, our Lord and God,
> to receive glory and honor and power,
for you created all things,
> and by your will they were created
> and have their being.

Intercessions

(Offer personal prayers.)

The Lord's Prayer

Dismissal

O Lord, remove our sin from your sight, show us the light of your countenance, and refresh us with the sense of your favor, through Jesus Christ, our Redeemer, to whom with you and the Holy Spirit, be all honor and praise forever and ever. Amen.

Personal Meditations

DAY 4 † Morning Prayer

O Lord, open my lips, and my mouth will declare your praise (Ps. 51:15).

Psalm 95:1-2

Come, let us sing for joy to the LORD;
    let us shout aloud to the Rock of our salvation.
Let us come before him with thanksgiving
    and extol him with music and song.

Glory to the Father, and to the Son, and to the Holy Spirit: as it was in the beginning, is now, and will be forever. Amen.

Hymn

The Lord is King, rejoice and sing;
    Our Lord and King thou art.
Thy Spirit reigns, thy love maintains
    Its sway within our hearts.

Psalm 36:5-7

Your love, O LORD, reaches to the heavens,
    your faithfulness to the skies.
Your righteousness is like the mighty mountains,
    your justice like the great deep.
O LORD, you preserve both man and beast.
    How priceless is your unfailing love!

Prayer

O God, blessed forever, we thank and praise you for all your benefits, for the comforts of this life, and our hope of everlasting salvation in the life to come.

Psalm 47:1-2, 6-7

Clap your hands, all you nations;
    shout to God with cries of joy.
How awesome is the LORD Most High,
    the great King over all the earth!

. . . .

Sing praises to God, sing praises;
  sing praises to our King, sing praises.
For God is the King of all the earth;
  sing to him a psalm of praise.

Prayer

O God, we desire to have a lively sense of your love always possessing our hearts, continually urging us to love you, obey you, and trust you.

Scripture Reading (Optional)   Matthew 7:12

Intercessions

With adoration and devotion to the One who dwells in the light that no person can approach, let us pray,

Send your Holy Spirit to be the Guide in all our ways.

Save, defend, and build us up in your fear and love; give to us the light of your countenance, peace from heaven, and the salvation of our souls in the day of the Lord Jesus.

Send your Holy Spirit to be the Guide in all our ways.

Give us grace to take up our cross daily—to accustom ourselves to bear hardship.

Send your Holy Spirit to be the Guide in all our ways.

Set a watch over our senses and appetites, our passions and understanding, that we may firmly deny satisfying them in any way that does not tend to your glory.

Send your Holy Spirit to be the Guide in all our ways.

(Offer personal prayers.)

The Lord's Prayer

Dismissal

Let these our prayers, O Lord, find access to the throne of grace, through the Son of your love, Jesus Christ the righteous; to whom, with you, O Father, in the unity of the Spirit, be all love and obedience now and forever. Amen.

DAY 4 † Evening Prayer

Self-Examination

(Reflect on the day, using the following questions as a guide, confess any departures from the law of love, and ask God for forgiveness.)

- Have I made up excuses to avoid self-denial?
- Have I submitted my will to the will of those opposing it, except where the glory of God was concerned?

Opening

O God, come to my assistance; O Lord, make haste to help me (Ps. 69:2, DRA).

Glory to the Father, and to the Son, and to the Holy Spirit: as it was in the beginning, is now, and will be forever. Amen.

Colossians 1:12-14

[Give] thanks to the Father, who has qualified you to share in the inheritance of the saints in the kingdom of light. For he has rescued us from the dominion of darkness and brought us into the kingdom of the Son he loves, in whom we have redemption, the forgiveness of sins.

Intercessions

(Offer personal prayers.)

The Lord's Prayer

Dismissal

Into your hand, O my God, we this night commend our souls and bodies. Grant us such rest and sleep as may fit us for the duties of the following day, through Jesus Christ our Lord. Amen.

Personal Meditations

DAY 5 † Morning Prayer

O Lord, open my lips, and my mouth will declare your praise (Ps. 51:15).

Psalm 95:6-7

Come, let us bow down in worship,
>let us kneel before the LORD our Maker;
for he is our God
>and we are the people of his pasture,
>the flock under his care.

Glory to the Father, and to the Son, and to the Holy Spirit: as it was in the beginning, is now, and will be forever. Amen.

Hymn

God of all pow'r, truth, and grace,
>*Which shall from age to age endure,*
Whose word, when heav'n and earth shall pass,
>*Remains and stands forever sure.*

Psalm 57:8-11

Awake, my soul!
>Awake, harp and lyre!
I will awaken the dawn.

I will praise you, O Lord, among the nations;
>I will sing of you among the peoples.
For great is your love, reaching to the heavens;
>your faithfulness reaches to the skies.

Be exalted, O God, above the heavens;
>let your glory be over all the earth.

Prayer

O Lord, upon you the eyes of all do wait, for you give to all life and breath and all things.

Psalm 46:1-3

God is our refuge and strength,
    an ever-present help in trouble.
Therefore we will not fear, though the earth give way
    and the mountains fall into the heart of the sea,
though its waters roar and foam
    and the mountains quake with their surging.

Prayer

O God of our salvation, you still watch over us for good and daily renew
to us our lives and your mercies.

Scripture Reading (Optional)   Isaiah 66:1-2

Intercessions

Trusting in the compassion of our all-sufficient God, let us pray,
        O Father of mercies, help us with your grace.
Direct our paths, and teach us to set you always before us.
        O Father of mercies, help us with your grace.
May whatever we do or suffer this day tend to your glory.
        O Father of mercies, help us with your grace.
We are not ours, but yours. Claim us as your right; keep us as your
charge; love us as your children.
        O Father of mercies, help us with your grace.

        (Offer personal prayers.)

The Lord's Prayer

Dismissal

Let your grace, O Lord Jesus, your love, O Heavenly Father, and your
comforting fellowship, O blessed Spirit, be with us, and with all that
desire our prayers, this day and forevermore. Amen.

DAY 5 † Evening Prayer

Self-Examination

(Reflect on the day, using the following questions as a guide, confess any departures from the law of love, and ask God for forgiveness.)

- Have I sought to will what God wills, and that only?
- Have I said anything with a stern look or manner, especially on religion?

Opening

O God, come to my assistance; O Lord, make haste to help me (Ps. 69:2, DRA).

Glory to the Father, and to the Son, and to the Holy Spirit: as it was in the beginning, is now, and will be forever. Amen.

Revelation 11:17-18

We give thanks to you, Lord God Almighty,
> the One who is and who was,
because you have taken your great power
> and have begun to reign.

Intercessions

(Offer personal prayers.)

The Lord's Prayer

Dismissal

Preserve us, O Lord, from everything hurtful, and let your merciful arms forever surround us, through Jesus Christ our Savior. Amen.

Personal Meditations

DAY 6 † Morning Prayer

O Lord, open my lips, and my mouth will declare your praise (Ps. 51:15).

Psalm 24:1-2

> The earth is the LORD's, and everything in it,
>> the world, and all who live in it;
> for he founded it upon the seas
>> and established it upon the waters.

Glory to the Father, and to the Son, and to the Holy Spirit: as it was in the beginning, is now, and will be forever. Amen.

Hymn

> *This is thy will, I know,*
>> *That I should holy be;*
> *Should let my sins this moment go,*
>> *This moment turn to thee.*

Psalm 51:1-2

> Have mercy on me, O God,
>> according to your unfailing love;
> according to your great compassion
>> blot out my transgressions.
> Wash away all my iniquity
>> and cleanse me from my sin.

Prayer

> O God, heal our backslidings, renew us to repentance, establish our hearts in your fear and love, and establish our steps in your way so that they do not slip.

Psalm 103:1-5

> Praise the LORD, O my soul;
>> all my inmost being, praise his holy name.
> Praise the LORD, O my soul,
>> and forget not all his benefits—

who forgives all your sins
>and heals all your diseases,
who redeems your life from the pit
>and crowns you with love and compassion,
who satisfies your desires with good things
>so that your youth is renewed like the eagle's.

Prayer

O God, now that you have renewed our lives and your mercies to us this morning, help us to renew our desires, resolutions, and efforts to live in obedience to your holy will.

Scripture Reading (Optional)   Ephesians 4:29-32

Intercessions

With adoration and gratitude to our Savior and Lord, let us pray,
>*Be our light and our peace.*

You are the brightness of your Father's glory, the express image of his person; you have destroyed the power of the devil and have overcome death.
>*Be our light and our peace.*

Destroy the power of the devil in us and make us new creatures; cast out of our hearts all corrupt inclinations.
>*Be our light and our peace.*

Heal the disease of our souls, open our eyes and fix them solely on the prize of our high calling, and cleanse our hearts from every desire but that of advancing your glory.
>*Be our light and our peace.*

>*(Offer personal prayers.)*

The Lord's Prayer

Dismissal

Hear, O merciful Father, our prayers, for the sake of your Son Jesus, and bring us, with all those who have pleased you, into the glories of your Son's kingdom, to whom with you and the Holy Spirit be all praise forever and ever. Amen.

DAY 6 † Evening Prayer

Self-Examination

(Reflect on the day, using the following questions as a guide, confess any departures from the law of love, and ask God for forgiveness.)

- Have I considered any opportunity to practice self-denial too small to undertake?
- Have I set apart some time to gain an intense awareness of Christ's suffering and my sins?

Opening

O God, come to my assistance; O Lord, make haste to help me (Ps. 69:2, DRA).

Glory to the Father, and to the Son, and to the Holy Spirit: as it was in the beginning, is now, and will be forever. Amen.

Revelation 15:3

Great and marvelous are your deeds,
> Lord God Almighty.
Just and true are your ways,
> King of the ages.

Intercessions

(Offer personal prayers.)

The Lord's Prayer

Dismissal

And now, O Lord my God, take us under your protection this night and preserve us from all evil. These and all other mercies we humbly request in the name or our Mediator, Jesus Christ. Amen.

Personal Meditations

DAY 7 † Morning Prayer

O Lord, open my lips, and my mouth will declare your praise (Ps. 51:15).

Psalm 67:1-2

May God be gracious to us and bless us
  and make his face shine upon us,
      Selah
that your ways may be known on earth,
  your salvation among all nations.

Glory to the Father, and to the Son, and to the Holy Spirit: as it was in the beginning, is now, and will be forever. Amen.

Hymn

O God of all grace, your goodness we praise;
your Son you have given to die in our place.
he came from above our curse to remove;
he has loved, he has loved us because he would love.

Psalm 119:145-147

I call with all my heart; answer me, O LORD,
  and I will obey your decrees.
I call out to you; save me
  and I will keep your statutes.
I rise before dawn and cry for help;
  I have put my hope in your word.

Prayer

O God, mercifully accept this our morning sacrifice of praise and thanksgiving.

Psalm 117

Praise the LORD, all you nations;
>   extol him, all you peoples.
For great is his love toward us,
>   and the faithfulness of the LORD endures forever.
>   Praise the LORD.

Prayer

O Lord, pour your grace into our hearts that we may worthily magnify your great and glorious name.

Scripture Reading (Optional)   2 Peter 1:10-11

Intercessions

With all humility, let us lift up our hearts to our great Creator and Sovereign Lord, praying,
>   *Help us, O Father, to fulfill the end of our creation.*
You have made us and sent us into the world to do your work.
>   *Help us, O Father, to fulfill the end of our creation.*
Guide us by your Holy Spirit in all those places where you will lead us this day, and do not let our interaction with the world make us inattentive to your presence or lukewarm in your service.
>   *Help us, O Father, to fulfill the end of our creation.*
Allow whatever we undertake this day to succeed in tending to your glory, the good of our neighbor, and the salvation of our souls.
>   *Help us, O Father, to fulfill the end of our creation.*

>   *(Offer personal prayers.)*

The Lord's Prayer

Dismissal

O Father, renew us daily with your Holy Spirit and guide us in all your ways till you have perfected us for your heavenly kingdom, through Jesus Christ, our Savior and Redeemer. Amen.

DAY 7 † Evening Prayer

Self-Examination

(Reflect on the day, using the following questions as a guide, confess any departures from the law of love, and ask God for forgiveness.)

- Have I set aside some time for thanking God for the blessings of the past week?
- Have I considered each of them as a call to a greater love and, thus, to a more faithful holiness?

Opening

O God, come to my assistance; O Lord, make haste to help me (Ps. 69:2, DRA).

Glory to the Father, and to the Son, and to the Holy Spirit: as it was in the beginning, is now, and will be forever. Amen.

Philippians 2:6-7

[Jesus], being in very nature God,
　did not consider equality with God something to be grasped,
but made himself nothing,
　taking the very nature of a servant,
　being made in human likeness.

Intercessions

(Offer personal prayers.)

The Lord's Prayer

Dismissal

O Father, under the shadow of your wings let us pass this night in comfort and peace. We ask this in the name of your dear Son, our Savior, Jesus Christ. Amen.

Personal Meditations

DAY 8 † Morning Prayer

Psalm 67:3-4

> May the peoples praise you, O God;
>> may all the peoples praise you.
> May the nations be glad and sing for joy,
>> for you rule the peoples justly
>> and guide the nations of the earth.

Glory to the Father, and to the Son, and to the Holy Spirit: as it was in the beginning, is now, and will be forever. Amen.

Hymn

> *Love divine, all loves excelling,*
>> *Joy of heav'n, to earth come down!*
> *Fix in us your humble dwelling;*
>> *All your faithful mercies crown.*

Psalm 118:1-4

> Give thanks to the LORD, for he is good;
>> his love endures forever.
> Let Israel say:
>> "His love endures forever."
> Let the house of Aaron say:
>> "His love endures forever."
> Let those who fear the LORD say:
>> "His love endures forever."

Prayer

> Almighty God, we present ourselves, with all humility, before you, to offer our morning sacrifice of love and thanksgiving.

Psalm 150:1-3, 6

Praise the LORD.
Praise God in his sanctuary;
    praise him in his mighty heavens.
Praise him for his acts of power;
    praise him for his surpassing greatness.
Praise him with the sounding of the trumpet,
    praise him with the harp and lyre.

. . . .

Let everything that has breath praise the LORD.

Prayer

O eternal God, we bless you on behalf of all your creatures and acknowledge your priceless benefits bestowed on us in Christ Jesus.

Scripture Reading (Optional)   Ezekiel 36:25-28

Intercessions

Let us lift up our hearts in praise and thanksgiving to our Savior and Lord, praying,

Glory to you, O holy Jesus.

You offered yourself a full, perfect, and sufficient sacrifice for the sins of the whole world.

Glory to you, O holy Jesus.

You rose again the third day from the dead and had all power given to you both in heaven and on earth.

Glory to you, O holy Jesus.

Take full possession of our hearts, and make us like you—all kindness, goodness, gentleness, meekness, and longsuffering.

Glory to you, O holy Jesus.

(Offer personal prayers.)

The Lord's Prayer

Dismissal

O Lord God, fill us with a comforting and sustaining sense of your presence throughout this day, through Jesus Christ. Amen.

DAY 8 † Evening Prayer

Self-Examination

(Reflect on the day, using the following questions as a guide, confess any departures from the law of love, and ask God for forgiveness.)

- Have I taken time to think about God's love and mercy?
- Have I unnecessarily mentioned the failings or faults of anyone?

Opening

O God, come to my assistance; O Lord, make haste to help me (Ps. 69:2, DRA).

Glory to the Father, and to the Son, and to the Holy Spirit: as it was in the beginning, is now, and will be forever. Amen.

Revelation 19:5

Praise our God,
    all you his servants,
you who fear him,
    both small and great!

Intercessions

(Offer personal prayers.)

The Lord's Prayer

Dismissal

O Father, protect us and all our friends everywhere this night; and awaken in the morning those good thoughts in our hearts, that the words of our Savior may abide in us and we in him. Through Jesus Christ our Lord, we pray. Amen.

Personal Meditations

DAY 9 † Morning Prayer

O Lord, open my lips, and my mouth will declare your praise (Ps. 51:15).

Psalm 67:5-7

May the peoples praise you, O God;
    may all the peoples praise you.
Then the land will yield its harvest,
    and God, our God, will bless us.
God will bless us,
    and all the ends of the earth will fear him.

Glory to the Father, and to the Son, and to the Holy Spirit: as it was in the beginning, is now, and will be forever. Amen.

Hymn

Christ, whose glory fills the skies;
    Christ, the true, the only Light;
Sun of Righteousness, arise,
    Triumph o'er the shades of night.

Psalm 42:1-3, 5-6

As the deer pants for streams of water,
    so my soul pants for you, O God.
My soul thirsts for God, for the living God.
    When can I go and meet with God?
My tears have been my food
    day and night,
while men say to me all day long,
    "Where is your God?"

    . . . .

Why are you downcast, O my soul?
    Why so disturbed within me?
Put your hope in God,
    for I will yet praise him,
    my Savior and my God.

Prayer

O our God, fill our souls with so entire a love of you that we may love
nothing but for your sake.

Psalm 19:1-4

The heavens declare the glory of God;
the skies proclaim the work of his hands.
Day after day they pour forth speech;
night after night they display knowledge.
There is no speech or language
where their voice is not heard.
Their voice goes out into all the earth,
their words to the ends of the world.

Prayer

O Lord, adored be your goodness for the good things of this life and the
hope of eternal happiness.

Scripture Reading (Optional)   Jeremiah 15:16

Intercessions

To the One who extends his loving-kindness to all humanity, let us pray,
O Lord, make us the pattern of your love.
Let us treat all our neighbors with that tender love due to your children.
O Lord, make us the pattern of your love.
Grant that we may assist all our brothers and sisters with our prayers
when we cannot reach them with actual services.
O Lord, make us the pattern of your love.
Make us zealous to take every opportunity to assist the needy, protect the
oppressed, instruct the ignorant, and steady the wavering.
O Lord, make us the pattern of your love.

(Offer personal prayers.)

The Lord's Prayer

Dismissal

O Lord God, help us to serve you and bring forth many good works
throughout all our lives, through Jesus Christ. Amen.

DAY 9 † Evening Prayer

Self-Examination

(Reflect on the day, using the following questions as a guide, confess any departures from the law of love, and ask God for forgiveness.)

- Was I determined to do all the good I could today?
- Have I disagreed with anyone without a good reason or when there was no chance of convincing?

Opening

O God, come to my assistance; O Lord, make haste to help me (Ps. 69:2, DRA).

Glory to the Father, and to the Son, and to the Holy Spirit: as it was in the beginning, is now, and will be forever. Amen.

Ephesians 1:4

[God] chose us in [Christ] before the creation of the world to be holy and blameless in his sight.

Intercessions

(Offer personal prayers.)

The Lord's Prayer

Dismissal

O Father in heaven, refresh us with such comforting rest that we may rise more fit for your service, through Jesus Christ, our Savior and Redeemer. Amen.

Personal Meditations

DAY 10 † Morning Prayer

O Lord, open my lips, and my mouth will declare your praise (Ps. 51:15).

Psalm 24:3-5

Who may ascend the hill of the LORD?
 Who may stand in his holy place?
He who has clean hands and a pure heart,
 who does not lift up his soul to an idol
 or swear by what is false.
He will receive blessing from the LORD
 and vindication from God his Savior.

Glory to the Father, and to the Son, and to the Holy Spirit: as it was in the beginning, is now, and will be forever. Amen.

Hymn

Let earth and hell their pow'rs engage,
 And fierce temptations rise;
Above their impotence of rage,
 My soul to Jesus flies.

Psalm 56:1-4

Be merciful to me, O God, for men hotly pursue me;
 all day long they press their attack.
My slanderers pursue me all day long;
 many are attacking me in their pride.
When I am afraid,
 I will trust in you.
In God, whose word I praise,
 in God I trust; I will not be afraid.
 What can mortal man do to me?

Prayer

O Father, accompany us all this day with your blessing so that we may please you in body and soul and be safe under your defense.

Psalm 65:1-4

Praise awaits you, O God, in Zion;
   to you our vows will be fulfilled.
O you who hear prayer,
   to you all men will come.
When we were overwhelmed by sins,
   you forgave our transgressions.
Blessed are those you choose
   and bring near to live in your courts!

Prayer

O blessed Lord, enable us to fulfill all your commands.

Scripture Reading (Optional)   1 Thessalonians 5:2-6

Intercessions

With hearts filled with love and adoration for Christ, our merciful
Redeemer, let us pray,

   O Savior, pour into us the whole spirit of humility.

Do with us what seems best in your own eyes; only give us the mind that
was in you; let us learn from you to be meek and lowly.

   O Savior, pour into us the whole spirit of humility.

Save us from desiring or seeking the honor that comes from other people.

   O Savior, pour into us the whole spirit of humility.

When the cords of pride overtake us, do not allow us to take pleasure in
them, but enable us to instantly flee to you.

   O Savior, pour into us the whole spirit of humility.

   (Offer personal prayers.)

The Lord's Prayer

Dismissal

O Heavenly Father, help us this day to do everything you have com-
manded us to do wholeheartedly, with goodwill, and with true love for
your service, through Jesus Christ our Lord. Amen.

DAY 10 † Evening Prayer

Self-Examination

(Reflect on the day, using the following questions as a guide, confess any departures from the law of love, and ask God for forgiveness.)

- Have I set apart some time this day to think about my weaknesses and sins?
- Have I desired the praise of others?

Opening

O God, come to my assistance; O Lord, make haste to help me (Ps. 69:2, DRA).

Glory to the Father, and to the Son, and to the Holy Spirit: as it was in the beginning, is now, and will be forever. Amen.

Revelation 5:9

You are worthy [O Lamb] to take the scroll
    and to open its seals,
because you were slain,
    and with your blood you purchased men for God
from every tribe and language and people and nation.

Intercessions

(Offer personal prayers.)

The Lord's Prayer

Dismissal

O merciful Father, grant that we and all the members of your holy church may find mercy in the day of judgment, through the mediation and satisfaction of your blessed Son, Jesus Christ; to whom, with you and the Holy Spirit, be all honor and praise forever. Amen.

Personal Meditations

DAY 11 † Morning Prayer

> O Lord, open my lips, and my mouth will declare your praise (Ps. 51:15).

Psalm 100:1-2

Shout for joy to the LORD, all the earth.
>Worship the LORD with gladness;
>come before him with joyful songs.

Glory to the Father, and to the Son, and to the Holy Spirit: as it was in the beginning, is now, and will be forever. Amen.

Hymn

Glory be to God above,
>*God from whom all blessings flow;*
Make we mention of his love,
>*Publish we his praise below.*

Psalm 77:13-15

Your ways, O God, are holy.
>What god is so great as our God?
You are the God who performs miracles;
>you display your power among the peoples.
With your mighty arm you redeemed your people,
>the descendants of Jacob and Joseph.

Prayer

O God, we thank you for all the good things you have given to the whole world, especially to us whom you have called to the knowledge of your grace in Christ Jesus.

Psalm 97:10-12

Let those who love the LORD hate evil,
> for he guards the lives of his faithful ones
> and delivers them from the hand of the wicked.

Light is shed upon the righteous
> and joy on the upright in heart.

Rejoice in the LORD, you who are righteous,
> and praise his holy name.

Prayer

O Lord God, let your mighty power enable us to do our duty toward you and toward all people, with care, diligence, zeal, and perseverance to the end.

Scripture Reading (Optional) Romans 8:35-39

Intercessions

To the One who is the Way, the Truth, and the Life, let us lift up our hearts in love and humble adoration, praying,

> *O Savior, help us to deny ourselves and follow you.*

You emptied yourself of your eternal glory and took upon yourself the form of a servant.

> *O Savior, help us to deny ourselves and follow you.*

You allowed your cheeks to be struck, your back to be scourged, and your hands and feet to be nailed to an accursed tree; you renounced yourself.

> *O Savior, help us to deny ourselves and follow you.*

Let us not presume to be above you, our great Master. Let there be one desire of our hearts, to be as you are—to do, not our own will, but the will of him who sent us.

> *O Savior, help us to deny ourselves and follow you.*

> *(Offer personal prayers.)*

The Lord's Prayer

Dismissal

O Heavenly Father, let your grace always surround us so that we may be continually given to all good works and may always glorify you. Amen.

DAY 11 † Evening Prayer

Self-Examination

(Reflect on the day, using the following questions as a guide, confess any departures from the law of love, and ask God for forgiveness.)

- Have I put my own desires ahead of those of others?
- Have I avoided helping someone because I didn't want to spare the time?

Opening

O God, come to my assistance; O Lord, make haste to help me (Ps. 69:2, DRA).

Glory to the Father, and to the Son, and to the Holy Spirit: as it was in the beginning, is now, and will be forever. Amen.

Colossians 1:15-16

[The Son] is the image of the invisible God, the firstborn over all creation. For by him all things were created: things in heaven and on earth, visible and invisible, whether thrones or powers or rulers or authorities; all things were created by him and for him.

Intercessions

(Offer personal prayers.)

The Lord's Prayer

Dismissal

These my prayers, O most merciful Father, graciously hear, through the mediation of Jesus Christ, our Redeemer, who with you and the Holy Spirit is worshipped and glorified in all the churches of the saints, one God blessed forever. Amen.

Personal Meditations

DAY 12 † Morning Prayer

O Lord, open my lips, and my mouth will declare your praise (Ps. 51:15).

Psalm 100:3

Know that the LORD is God.
It is he who made us, and we are his;
we are his people, the sheep of his pasture.

Glory to the Father, and to the Son, and to the Holy Spirit: as it was in the beginning, is now, and will be forever. Amen.

Hymn

Sing with glad anticipation,
*   Mortals and immortals sing;*
Jesus comes with full salvation,
*   Jesus doth his glory bring.*
Hallelujah, Hallelujah,
*   God omnipotent is King!*

Psalm 80:1-3

Hear us, O Shepherd of Israel,
    you who lead Joseph like a flock;
you who sit enthroned between the cherubim, shine forth
    before Ephraim, Benjamin and Manasseh.
Awaken your might;
    come and save us.

Restore us, O God;
    make your face shine upon us,
    that we may be saved.

Prayer

O eternal God, we humbly and heartily thank you for redeeming us by the death of your blessed Son and for the assistance of your Holy Spirit.

Psalm 121:1-4

I lift up my eyes to the hills—
> where does my help come from?
My help comes from the LORD,
> the Maker of heaven and earth.
He will not let your foot slip—
> he who watches over you will not slumber;
indeed, he who watches over Israel
> will neither slumber nor sleep.

Prayer

O Lord, give us such a sense of your infinite goodness that we may
return to you all possible love and obedience.

Scripture Reading (Optional)   Romans 14:1-21

Intercessions

With unreserved love and commitment to our Creator, Redeemer, and
Sanctifier, let us pray,

> *We give ourselves up entirely to you.*

We give you our understanding. May it be our foremost care to know
you, your perfections, your works, and your will.

> *We give ourselves up entirely to you*

We give you our will. May we will your glory in all things, as you do, and
make that our goal in everything.

> *We give ourselves up entirely to you.*

We give you the inclinations of our hearts. Be our love, our fear, and our
joy. Moreover, what you love, may we love; what you hate, may we hate.

> *We give ourselves up entirely to you.*

> *(Offer personal prayers.)*

The Lord's Prayer

Dismissal

O Lord, graciously keep us this day from all sin. Bless our going out and
coming in, now and forevermore. Amen.

DAY 12 † Evening Prayer

Self-Examination

(Reflect on the day, using the following questions as a guide, confess any departures from the law of love, and ask God for forgiveness.)

- Have I (after doing what he requires me to do about them) left all future things totally to God's handling?
- Have I resumed my claim to my body, soul, friends, fame, or fortune after I gave it to God?

Opening

O God, come to my assistance; O Lord, make haste to help me (Ps. 69:2, DRA).

Glory to the Father, and to the Son, and to the Holy Spirit: as it was in the beginning, is now, and will be forever. Amen.

Revelation 12:10

Now have come the salvation and the power and the kingdom of our God,
and the authority of his Christ.
For the accuser of our brothers,
who accuses them before our God day and night,
has been hurled down.

Intercessions

(Offer personal prayers.)

The Lord's Prayer

Dismissal

O Lord our God, grant us an abundant entrance into your everlasting kingdom, through Jesus Christ, our Lord and Savior. Amen.

Personal Meditations

DAY 13 † Morning Prayer

O Lord, open my lips, and my mouth will declare your praise (Ps. 51:15).

Psalm 100:4-5

Enter [the LORD's] gates with thanksgiving
and his courts with praise;
give thanks to him and praise his name.
For the LORD is good and his love endures forever;
his faithfulness continues through all generations.

Glory to the Father, and to the Son, and to the Holy Spirit: as it was in the beginning, is now, and will be forever. Amen.

Hymn

And can it be that I should gain
An int'rest in the Savior's blood?
Died he for me, who caused his pain?
For me, who him to death pursued?

Amazing love! How can it be
That thou, my God, shouldst die for me?

Psalm 51:7-9

Cleanse me with hyssop, [O God,] and I will be clean;
wash me, and I will be whiter than snow.
Let me hear joy and gladness;
let the bones you have crushed rejoice.
Hide your face from my sins
and blot out all my iniquity.

Prayer

O Lord our God, lead us to the fountain opened for sin and uncleanness so that we may wash and be cleansed.

Psalm 147:7-11

Sing to the LORD with thanksgiving;
make music to our God on the harp.

He covers the sky with clouds;
> he supplies the earth with rain
> and makes grass grow on the hills.
He provides food for the cattle
> and for the young ravens when they call.
His pleasure is not in the strength of the horse,
> nor his delight in the legs of a man;
the LORD delights in those who fear him,
> who put their hope in his unfailing love.

Prayer

O Lord, now that you have renewed us and your mercies to us, restrain us from the sins into which we are most prone to fall and urge us on to the duties we are most averse to perform.

Scripture Reading (Optional)   Ephesians 2:13-16

Intercessions

With humility and wholehearted devotion, let us lift up our hearts to our beloved Lord and Savior, praying,

> *Lord, make us more like you.*

O Jesus, poor and abject, unknown and despised, have mercy on us and let us not be ashamed to follow you.

> *Lord, make us more like you.*

O Jesus, clothed with a habit of reproach and shame, have mercy on us and let us not seek our own glory.

> *Lord, make us more like you.*

O Jesus, hanging on the tree, bowing the head, giving up the ghost, have mercy on us and conform us to your holy, humble, suffering Spirit.

> *Lord, make us more like you.*

> *(Offer personal prayers.)*

The Lord's Prayer

Dismissal

Be with us, O Lord, this day, to bless and keep. Guide and govern us, and let us be yours and only yours forever. Amen.

DAY 13 † Evening Prayer

Self-Examination

(Reflect on the day, using the following questions as a guide, confess any departures from the law of love, and ask God for forgiveness.)

- Have I looked to God as my Good, my Pattern, and my one Desire?
- Have I been zealous to do and active in doing good?

Opening

O God, come to my assistance; O Lord, make haste to help me (Ps. 69:2, DRA).

Glory to the Father, and to the Son, and to the Holy Spirit: as it was in the beginning, is now, and will be forever. Amen.

Revelation 15:4

Who will not fear you, O Lord,
   and bring glory to your name?
For you alone are holy.
All nations will come
   and worship before you,
for your righteous acts have been revealed.

Intercessions

(Offer personal prayers.)

The Lord's Prayer

Dismissal

O blessed God, give us comfortable sleep to strengthen us for your service, through Jesus Christ our Lord. Amen.

Personal Meditations

DAY 14 † Morning Prayer

> O Lord, open my lips, and my mouth will declare your praise (Ps. 51:15).

Psalm 95:1-2

Come, let us sing for joy to the LORD;
    let us shout aloud to the Rock of our salvation.
Let us come before him with thanksgiving
    and extol him with music and song.

Glory to the Father, and to the Son, and to the Holy Spirit: as it was in the beginning, is now, and will be forever. Amen.

Hymn

Glory be to God on high,
    And peace on earth descend;
God comes down, he bows the sky,
    And shows himself our Friend.

Psalm 92:1-3

It is good to praise the LORD
    and make music to your name, O Most High,
to proclaim your love in the morning
    and your faithfulness at night,
to the music of the ten-stringed lyre
    and the melody of the harp.

Prayer

Day by day we magnify you, O Lord, who makes every day an addition to your mercies.

Psalm 8:1, 3-5

O LORD, our Lord,
    how majestic is your name in all the earth!

. . . .

When I consider your heavens,
    the work of your fingers,

the moon and the stars,
   which you have set in place,
what is man that you are mindful of him,
   the son of man that you care for him?
You made him a little lower than the heavenly beings
   and crowned him with glory and honor.

Prayer

O Lord, we bless you for our creation, preservation, and, above all, for our redemption by our Lord and Savior Jesus Christ.

Scripture Reading (Optional)   Romans 12:13-21

Intercessions

With utter devotion to the Giver of life and Protector of all creatures, let us pray,

Pour your grace into our hearts, Lord.

Help us to worthily magnify your great and glorious name.

Pour your grace into our hearts, Lord.

Preserve us from all those snares and temptations that continually urge us to offend you.

Pour your grace into our hearts, Lord.

Keep us undefiled and blameless to the end; and grant that we may diligently perform your will in whatever place or position you have been pleased to place us.

Pour your grace into our hearts, Lord.

(Offer personal prayers.)

The Lord's Prayer

Dismissal

O Lord our God, help us today to see your power, to own your presence, to admire your wisdom, and to love your goodness in all your creatures, through Jesus Christ our Savior. Amen.

DAY 14 † Evening Prayer

Self-Examination

(Reflect on the day, using the following questions as a guide, confess any departures from the law of love, and ask God for forgiveness.)

- Have I daily thanked God for my creation, preservation, and all the other blessings he has poured down on me?
- Have I prayed regularly for God's holy Church and for all pastors and their families?

Opening

O God, come to my assistance; O Lord, make haste to help me (Ps. 69:2, DRA).

Glory to the Father, and to the Son, and to the Holy Spirit: as it was in the beginning, is now, and will be forever. Amen.

Philippians 2:8

And being found in appearance as a man,
[Jesus] humbled himself
and became obedient to death—even death on a cross!

Intercessions

(Offer personal prayers.)

The Lord's Prayer

Dismissal

O Father, keep us both in body and soul, and give us such rest as our bodies have need of, through Jesus Christ our Lord. Amen.

Personal Meditations

DAY 15 † Morning Prayer

> O Lord, open my lips, and my mouth will declare your praise (Ps. 51:15).

Psalm 95:6-7

Come, let us bow down in worship,
    let us kneel before the LORD our Maker;
for he is our God
    and we are the people of his pasture,
    the flock under his care.

Glory to the Father, and to the Son, and to the Holy Spirit: as it was in the beginning, is now, and will be forever. Amen.

Hymn

Being of beings! May our praise
    Your courts with grateful fragrance fill.
Still may we stand before your face,
    Still hear and do your sov'reign will.

Psalm 93:1-2

The LORD reigns, he is robed in majesty;
    the LORD is robed in majesty
    and is armed with strength.
The world is firmly established;
    it cannot be moved.
Your throne was established long ago;
    you are from all eternity.

Prayer

O Lord God, we ascribe all praise and glory to you, to whom alone it is due.

Psalm 148:1-6

Praise the LORD.
Praise the LORD from the heavens,
    praise him in the heights above.

Praise him, all his angels,
> praise him, all his heavenly hosts.

Praise him, sun and moon,
> praise him, all you shining stars.

Praise him, you highest heavens
> and you waters above the skies.

Let them praise the name of the LORD,
> for he commanded and they were created.

He set them in place for ever and ever;
> he gave a decree that will never pass away.

Prayer

Eternal God, we praise your holy name for so graciously raising us up, in soundness of body and mind, to see the light of this day.

Scripture Reading (Optional)   Ezekiel 37:12-14

Intercessions

Let us lift up our hearts in thankful praise to the Holy Spirit, praying,
> *Glory to you, O blessed Spirit.*

You came down in fiery tongues on the apostles and enabled them to preach the good news of salvation to a sinful world.
> *Glory to you, O blessed Spirit.*

Descend on us that we may be in the Spirit this day and always.
> *Glory to you, O blessed Spirit.*

Blessed be your goodness that we have felt you so often in our hearts, inspiring us with holy thoughts and filling us with love, joy, and comforting expectations of "the glory that shall be revealed."
> *Glory to you, O blessed Spirit.*

> *(Offer personal prayers.)*

The Lord's Prayer

Dismissal

O Lord, make it our delight throughout this day to praise you, to recall your loving-kindness, and to offer you the sacrifice of thanksgiving. Amen.

DAY 15 † Evening Prayer

Self-Examination

(Reflect on the day, using the following questions as a guide, confess any departures from the law of love, and ask God for forgiveness.)

- Have I faithfully gathered with other Christians for worship?
- Have I prayed daily with fervor and focus in my personal devotions?

Opening

O God, come to my assistance; O Lord, make haste to help me (Ps. 69:2, DRA).

Glory to the Father, and to the Son, and to the Holy Spirit: as it was in the beginning, is now, and will be forever. Amen.

Revelation 19:6-7

Hallelujah!
    For our Lord God Almighty reigns.
Let us rejoice and be glad
    and give him glory!
For the wedding of the Lamb has come,
    and his bride has made herself ready.

Intercessions

(Offer personal prayers.)

The Lord's Prayer

Dismissal

Take us, O God, into your gracious care and protection, through Jesus Christ our Lord. Amen.

Personal Meditations

DAY 16 † Morning Prayer

O Lord, open my lips, and my mouth will declare your praise (Ps. 51:15).

Psalm 24:1-2

The earth is the LORD's, and everything in it,
    the world, and all who live in it;
for he founded it upon the seas
    and established it upon the waters.

Glory to the Father, and to the Son, and to the Holy Spirit: as it was in the beginning, is now, and will be forever. Amen.

Hymn

O God, what off'ring shall I give
    To thee, the Lord of earth and skies?
My spirit, soul, and flesh receive,
    A holy, living sacrifice.

Psalm 84:1-4

How lovely is your dwelling place,
    O LORD Almighty!
My soul yearns, even faints,
    for the courts of the LORD;
my heart and my flesh cry out
    for the living God.

Even the sparrow has found a home,
    and the swallow a nest for herself,
    where she may have her young—
a place near your altar,
    O LORD Almighty, my King and my God.
Blessed are those who dwell in your house;
    they are ever praising you.

Prayer

O Lord God, we praise and bless your holy name for all your goodness and loving-kindness to us and all humanity.

Psalm 96:1-3

Sing to the LORD a new song;
>   sing to the LORD, all the earth.
Sing to the LORD, praise his name;
>   proclaim his salvation day after day.
Declare his glory among the nations,
>   his marvelous deeds among all peoples.

Prayer

O Father of all mercies, we bless you for your great love in the redemption of the world by our Lord Jesus Christ.

Scripture Reading (Optional)   James 2:12-13

Intercessions

With humility and devotion to the Lord of heaven and earth, let us pray,
>   *May we abound in your love more and more.*
We desire to be holy and undefiled as our blessed Master was, and we trust that you will fulfill all his gracious promises to us.
>   *May we abound in your love more and more.*
Guide and assist us in all our thoughts, words, and actions. Make us willing to do and suffer what you will.
>   *May we abound in your love more and more.*
As you inspire us with these desires, so accompany them always with your grace that we may every day, with our whole hearts, give ourselves up to your service.
>   *May we abound in your love more and more.*

>   *(Offer personal prayers.)*

The Lord's Prayer

Dismissal

Almighty Father, guide us safely throughout this day with a lively sense of your love to us, through Jesus Christ our Savior. Amen.

DAY 16 † Evening Prayer

Self-Examination

(Reflect on the day, using the following questions as a guide, confess any departures from the law of love, and ask God for forgiveness.)

- Have I sought to glorify God by every thought of my heart, every word of my tongue, and every work of my hand?
- Have I been zealous to pray for, procure, and promote the well-being of my neighbor?

Opening

O God, come to my assistance; O Lord, make haste to help me (Ps. 69:2, DRA).

Glory to the Father, and to the Son, and to the Holy Spirit: as it was in the beginning, is now, and will be forever. Amen.

Ephesians 1:4-6

In love [God] predestined us to be adopted as his sons through Jesus Christ, in accordance with his pleasure and will—to the praise of his glorious grace, which he has freely given us in the One he loves.

Intercessions

(Offer personal prayers.)

The Lord's Prayer

Dismissal

Father, grant to our bodies rest in bed and our souls rest in yourself, through Jesus Christ our Lord. Amen.

Personal Meditations

DAY 17 † Morning Prayer

> O Lord, open my lips, and my mouth will declare your praise (Ps. 51:15).

Psalm 67:1-2

May God be gracious to us and bless us
    and make his face shine upon us,
        Selah
that your ways may be known on earth,
    your salvation among all nations.

Glory to the Father, and to the Son, and to the Holy Spirit: as it was in the beginning, is now, and will be forever. Amen.

Hymn

Jesus the Lord has set us free,
Redeemed from all iniquity,
And raised his servants into sons,
We have redemption through His blood.

Psalm 85:8-13

I will listen to what God the LORD will say;
    he promises peace to his people, his saints—
    but let them not return to folly.
Surely his salvation is near those who fear him,
    that his glory may dwell in our land.

Love and faithfulness meet together;
    righteousness and peace kiss each other.
Faithfulness springs forth from the earth,
    and righteousness looks down from heaven.
The LORD will indeed give what is good,
    and our land will yield its harvest.
Righteousness goes before him
    and prepares the way for his steps.

Prayer

O Lord, because all the good done on earth is done by you, let us ever return to you all the glory.

Psalm 68:4-6

Sing to God, sing praise to his name,
  extol him who rides on the clouds—
his name is the LORD—
  and rejoice before him.
A father to the fatherless, a defender of widows,
  is God in his holy dwelling.
God sets the lonely in families,
  he leads forth the prisoners with singing;
  but the rebellious live in a sun-scorched land.

Prayer

O Father, we thank you for preserving us from our births to this moment.

Scripture Reading (Optional)   1 John 4:12-13

Intercessions

To our mighty Lord, the possessor of heaven and earth, let us pray,
  Father of mercies, hear our prayer.
You have said you will give your Holy Spirit to those who ask for it. Let it be to us according to your word.
  Father of mercies, hear our prayer.
Enable us to obey you with goodwill and true love to your service.
  Father of mercies, hear our prayer.
Incline us to be more and more in love with your laws, till they are written on our hearts.
  Father of mercies, hear our prayer.

  (Offer personal prayers.)

The Lord's Prayer

Dismissal

O God of all goodness, send down your heavenly grace into our souls so that today we will be able to worship and serve you as we should. Amen.

DAY 17 † Evening Prayer

Self-Examination

(Reflect on the day, using the following questions as a guide, confess any departures from the law of love, and ask God for forgiveness.)

- Have I avoided justifying myself when God's glory was not a concern?
- Have I spoken words that brought me praise when it was not essential to my neighbor's good?

Opening

O God, come to my assistance; O Lord, make haste to help me (Ps. 69:2, DRA).

Glory to the Father, and to the Son, and to the Holy Spirit: as it was in the beginning, is now, and will be forever. Amen

Revelation 5:12

Worthy is the Lamb, who was slain,
to receive power and wealth and wisdom and strength
and honor and glory and praise!

Intercessions

(Offer personal prayers.)

The Lord's Prayer

Dismissal

O God, raise up our spirits, together with our bodies, in the morning, to such a strong sense of your goodness that we will be motivated all day long in doing good, through Jesus Christ our Lord. Amen.

Personal Meditations

DAY 18 † Morning Prayer

> O Lord, open my lips, and my mouth will declare your praise (Ps. 51:15).

Psalm 67:3-4

May the peoples praise you, O God;
    may all the peoples praise you.
May the nations be glad and sing for joy,
    for you rule the peoples justly
    and guide the nations of the earth.

Glory to the Father, and to the Son, and to the Holy Spirit: as it was in the beginning, is now, and will be forever. Amen.

Hymn

Father, in whom we live,
    In whom we are, and move,
The glory, pow'r, and praise receive
    Of your creating love.

Psalm 86:1-4

Hear, O Lord, and answer me,
    for I am poor and needy.
Guard my life, for I am devoted to you.
    You are my God; save your servant
    who trusts in you.
Have mercy on me, O Lord,
    for I call to you all day long.
Bring joy to your servant,
    for to you, O Lord,
    I lift up my soul.

Prayer

Look upon us, O Lord, in your rich mercy, and for your dear Son's sake, be gracious to our souls.

Psalm 98:1-3

Sing to the LORD a new song,
  for he has done marvelous things;
his right hand and his holy arm
  have worked salvation for him.
The LORD has made his salvation known
  and revealed his righteousness to the nations.
He has remembered his love
  and his faithfulness to the house of Israel;
all the ends of the earth have seen
  the salvation of our God.

Prayer

O Lord, accept our sincere praise and thanksgiving for giving us everything we need to advance our present and eternal happiness.

Scripture Reading (Optional)   1 Timothy 6:6-10

Intercessions

To our saving Lord, who gave up his life and took it up again, let us pray,
  Help us to die to ourselves that we may live for you.
Unless we are buried together in the likeness of your death, we cannot rise in the likeness of your resurrection.
  Help us to die to ourselves that we may live for you.
Grant us grace to be dead to our own will and alive only to yours.
  Help us to die to ourselves that we may live for you.
Circumcise our hearts and make us new creatures so that it is no longer we who live but you who live in us.
  Help us to die to ourselves that we may live for you.

(Offer personal prayers.)

The Lord's Prayer

Dismissal

Guide us, good Father, and govern us throughout this day by your Holy Spirit, to whom with you and your Son, Jesus Christ, our Lord and Savior, be all glory, honor, and praise. Amen.

DAY 18 † Evening Prayer

Self-Examination

(Reflect on the day, using the following questions as a guide, confess any departures from the law of love, and ask God for forgiveness.)

- Have I been unkind in my treatment of others?
- Have I allowed the cares of the world to distract me from my devotion to God and my trust in his care?

Opening

O God, come to my assistance; O Lord, make haste to help me (Ps. 69:2, DRA).

Glory to the Father, and to the Son, and to the Holy Spirit: as it was in the beginning, is now, and will be forever. Amen.

Colossians 1:17

[Christ] is before all things, and in him all things hold together.

Intercessions

(Offer personal prayers.)

The Lord's Prayer

Dismissal

O God, our Creator and Preserver, keep us under the protection of your good care throughout this night. We ask this through Jesus Christ our Lord. Amen.

Personal Meditations

DAY 19 † Morning Prayer

O Lord, open my lips, and my mouth will declare your praise (Ps. 51:15).

Psalm 67:5-7

May the peoples praise you, O God;
>may all the peoples praise you.
Then the land will yield its harvest,
>and God, our God, will bless us.
God will bless us,
>and all the ends of the earth will fear him.

Glory to the Father, and to the Son, and to the Holy Spirit: as it was in the beginning, is now, and will be forever. Amen.

Hymn

Love, like death, hath all destroyed,
Rendered all distinctions void.
Names and sets and parties fall;
You, O Christ, are all in all.

Psalm 87:1-4

He has set his foundation on the holy mountain;
the LORD loves the gates of Zion
>more than all the dwellings of Jacob.
Glorious things are said of you,
>O city of God:
>> *Selah*
"I will record Rahab and Babylon
>among those who acknowledge me—
Philistia too, and Tyre, along with Cush—
>and will say, 'This one was born in Zion.'"

Prayer

O Lord our God, send your word to all the ends of the earth, and let it be the savor of life to all who hear it.

Psalm 99:1-3

The LORD reigns,
 let the nations tremble;
he sits enthroned between the cherubim,
 let the earth shake.
Great is the LORD in Zion;
 he is exalted over all the nations.
Let them praise your great and awesome name—
 he is holy.

Prayer

O Father, have mercy on all humanity. Draw all people to your truth.

Scripture Reading (Optional) 1 Peter 4:8-11

Intercessions

With unreserved love and commitment to our Lord and our God, let us pray,

We give ourselves up entirely to you.

We give you our bodies. May we glorify you with them and preserve them holy, fit for you to dwell in.

We give ourselves up entirely to you.

We give you all our worldly goods. May we prize them and use them only for you and be willing to part from them whenever you require them.

We give ourselves up entirely to you.

We give you our reputations. May we never value them but only as they relate to you.

We give ourselves up entirely to you.

(Offer personal prayers.)

The Lord's Prayer

Dismissal

O gracious Father, keep us this day in your favor and teach us in all our thoughts, words, and works to live to your glory, through Jesus Christ our Lord. Amen.

DAY 19 † Evening Prayer

Self-Examination

(Reflect on the day, using the following questions as a guide, confess any departures from the law of love, and ask God for forgiveness.)

- Have I allowed anything in this life to lessen my devotion and obedience to God?
- Have I been gracious and merciful to others even as God has been gracious and merciful to me?

Opening

O God, come to my assistance; O Lord, make haste to help me (Ps. 69:2, DRA).

Glory to the Father, and to the Son, and to the Holy Spirit: as it was in the beginning, is now, and will be forever. Amen.

Revelation 12:11

[Our brothers] overcame [their accuser]
by the blood of the Lamb
and by the word of their testimony;
they did not love their lives so much
as to shrink from death.

Intercessions

(Offer personal prayers.)

The Lord's Prayer

Dismissal

Take care of us this night, O Lord, and visit us with your mercies, through Jesus Christ. Amen.

Personal Meditations

DAY 20 † Morning Prayer

Psalm 24:3-5

Who may ascend the hill of the LORD?
   Who may stand in his holy place?
He who has clean hands and a pure heart,
   who does not lift up his soul to an idol
   or swear by what is false.
He will receive blessing from the LORD
   and vindication from God his Savior.

Glory to the Father, and to the Son, and to the Holy Spirit: as it was in the beginning, is now, and will be forever. Amen.

Hymn

O for a heart to praise my God,
   A heart from sin set free,
A heart that always feels your blood,
   So freely shed for me.

Psalm 51:10-12

Create in me a pure heart, O God,
   and renew a steadfast spirit within me.
Do not cast me from your presence
   or take your Holy Spirit from me.
Restore to me the joy of your salvation
   and grant me a willing spirit, to sustain me.

Prayer

O Lord, shed abroad in our hearts your love and fill us with all peace and joy in the Holy Spirit.

Psalm 105:1-4

Give thanks to the LORD, call on his name;
make known among the nations what he has done.
Sing to him, sing praise to him;
tell of all his wonderful acts.
Glory in his holy name;
let the hearts of those who seek the LORD rejoice.
Look to the LORD and his strength;
seek his face always.

Prayer

O Lord our God, let all our thoughts, words, and deeds be from now on to the glory of your great name.

Scripture Reading (Optional) 2 Corinthians 12:7-10

Intercessions

To our gracious and longsuffering heavenly Father, let us pray,

Lord, have mercy on us.

Be favorable to us as you always have been to those who love your holy name.

Lord, have mercy on us.

Forgive us when we sin and renew us to repentance, for the sake of your Son, Jesus, our Savior.

Lord, have mercy on us.

Let us no longer waver, no longer be weary or faint in our minds, no longer revolt from you or turn to folly again. May we go on conquering and to conquer all the hindrances to our salvation.

Lord, have mercy on us.

(Offer personal prayers.)

The Lord's Prayer

Dismissal

O Father, grant that today we may think, speak, and will and do the things befitting your children. In the name of Christ we pray. Amen.

DAY 20 † Evening Prayer

Self-Examination

(Reflect on the day, using the following questions as a guide, confess any departures from the law of love, and ask God for forgiveness.)

- Have I encouraged others in their Christian journey?
- Have I regularly prayed for family, friends, church, nation, and the world?

Opening

O God, come to my assistance; O Lord, make haste to help me (Ps. 69:2, DRA).

Glory to the Father, and to the Son, and to the Holy Spirit: as it was in the beginning, is now, and will be forever. Amen.

Revelation 4:8

Holy, holy, holy
is the Lord God Almighty,
who was, and is, and is to come.

Intercessions

(Offer personal prayers.)

The Lord's Prayer

Dismissal

O God, continue your fatherly care over us this night, through Jesus Christ our Lord. Amen.

Personal Meditations

DAY 21 † Morning Prayer

O Lord, open my lips, and my mouth will declare your praise (Ps. 51:15).

Psalm 100:1-2

Shout for joy to the LORD, all the earth.
Worship the LORD with gladness;
come before him with joyful songs.

Glory to the Father, and to the Son, and to the Holy Spirit: as it was in the beginning, is now, and will be forever. Amen.

Hymn

You, O Lord, I will obey;
You with vast delight pursue;
Walking in your pleasant way,
Glad your dear commands to do.

Psalm 119:149-151

Hear my voice in accordance with your love;
preserve my life, O LORD, according to your laws.
Those who devise wicked schemes are near,
but they are far from your law.
Yet you are near, O LORD,
and all your commands are true.

Prayer

Give us grace, O Lord, to keep your holy will and commandments all the days of our lives.

Psalm 113:1-3

Praise the LORD.
Praise, O servants of the LORD,
  praise the name of the LORD.
Let the name of the LORD be praised,
  both now and forevermore.
From the rising of the sun to the place where it sets,
  the name of the LORD is to be praised.

Prayer

We bless you, O Lord our God, for you are infinitely good and you have showed us what is good.

Scripture Reading (Optional)   Philippians 2:2-4

Intercessions

In wholehearted devotion we lift up our hearts to our heavenly Father, praying,

Watch over us with the eyes of your mercy.

Direct our souls and bodies according to the rule of your will that we may pass all our days to your glory.

Watch over us with the eyes of your mercy.

Give us understanding hearts to know and choose the good and hate and reject what is evil.

Watch over us with the eyes of your mercy.

Show us and make us what we must be before we can inherit your kingdom. Teach us the truth as it is in Jesus.

Watch over us with the eyes of your mercy.

(Offer personal prayers.)

The Lord's Prayer

Dismissal

O Lord our God, cause us to know the way we should go today and all the days of our lives, for we lift up our souls to you, through Jesus Christ our Savior. Amen.

DAY 21 † Evening Prayer

Self-Examination

(Reflect on the day, using the following questions as a guide, confess any departures from the law of love, and ask God for forgiveness.)

- Have I thanked God for his guidance and assistance in my daily tasks?
- Have I showed love to my enemies and prayed regularly for God to bless them?

Opening

O God, come to my assistance; O Lord, make haste to help me (Ps. 69:2, DRA).

Glory to the Father, and to the Son, and to the Holy Spirit: as it was in the beginning, is now, and will be forever. Amen.

Philippians 2:9

God exalted [Christ Jesus] to the highest place
and gave him the name that is above every name.

Intercessions

(Offer personal prayers.)

The Lord's Prayer

Dismissal

O God, make us to remember you in our beds and to think of you when we are waking, through Jesus Christ our Lord. Amen.

DAY 22 † Morning Prayer

O Lord, open my lips, and my mouth will declare your praise (Ps. 51:15).

Psalm 100:3

Know that the LORD is God.
>It is he who made us, and we are his;
>we are his people, the sheep of his pasture.

Glory to the Father, and to the Son, and to the Holy Spirit: as it was in the beginning, is now, and will be forever. Amen.

Hymn

All praise to God above,
>*In whom we have believed;*
The tokens of whose dying love
>*We have e'en now received.*

Psalm 118:17-24

I will not die but live,
>and will proclaim what the LORD has done.
The LORD has chastened me severely,
>but he has not given me over to death.

Open for me the gates of righteousness;
>I will enter and give thanks to the LORD.
This is the gate of the LORD
>through which the righteous may enter.
I will give you thanks, for you answered me;
>you have become my salvation.

The stone the builders rejected
>has become the capstone;
the LORD has done this,
>and it is marvelous in our eyes.
This is the day the LORD has made;
>let us rejoice and be glad in it.

Prayer

We give thanks to you, O God, for your marvelous love in Christ Jesus, by whom you have "reconciled the world to yourself."

Psalm 145:13-14

The LORD is faithful to all his promises
and loving toward all he has made.
The LORD upholds all those who fall
and lifts up all who are bowed down.

Prayer

We praise you, O God, for sealing your promises with the blood of Christ Jesus and confirming them with his resurrection, ascension, and the coming of the Holy Spirit.

Scripture Reading (Optional)   2 Timothy 2:8, 11-13

Intercessions

Let us lift up our hearts in praise and thanksgiving to our triune God, praying,

Glory to you, O holy, undivided Trinity.

You acted together in the great work of our redemption.

Glory to you, O holy, undivided Trinity.

You restored us again to the glorious liberty of the children of God.

Glory to you, O holy, undivided Trinity.

Let us ever esteem it our privilege and happiness to praise and love you.

Glory to you, O holy, undivided Trinity.

(Offer personal prayers.)

The Lord's Prayer

Dismissal

Accept this day, good Lord, all the praises of all your people, through Christ, our Savior and High Priest. Amen.

DAY 22 † Evening Prayer

Self-Examination

(Reflect on the day, using the following questions as a guide, confess any departures from the law of love, and ask God for forgiveness.)

- Have I been so intense in pursuing the tasks of earth that I have left little room for the things of heaven?
- Have I allowed my love for any creature to become greater than my love for God?

Opening

O God, come to my assistance; O Lord, make haste to help me (Ps. 69:2, DRA).

Glory to the Father, and to the Son, and to the Holy Spirit: as it was in the beginning, is now, and will be forever. Amen.

Hebrews 12:22-23

But you have come to Mount Zion, to the heavenly Jerusalem, the city of the living God. You have come to thousands upon thousands of angels in joyful assembly, to the church of the firstborn, whose names are written in heaven.

Intercessions

(Offer personal prayers.)

The Lord's Prayer

Dismissal

Preserve us, O God, from all dangers during the night, through Christ our Lord. Amen.

Personal Meditations

DAY 23 † Morning Prayer

O Lord, open my lips, and my mouth will declare your praise (Ps. 51:15).

Psalm 100:4-5

Enter [the LORD's] gates with thanksgiving
and his courts with praise;
give thanks to him and praise his name.
For the LORD is good and his love endures forever;
his faithfulness continues through all generations.

Glory to the Father, and to the Son, and to the Holy Spirit: as it was in the beginning, is now, and will be forever. Amen.

Hymn

In God's providential care
Ever intimately near,
All his various works declare
God, the bounteous God, is here.

Psalm 90:1-2

Lord, you have been our dwelling place
throughout all generations.
Before the mountains were born
or you brought forth the earth and the world,
from everlasting to everlasting you are God.

Prayer

O Lord, we bow ourselves before you, acknowledging we have nothing
but what we receive from you.

Psalm 135:1-6

Praise the LORD.
Praise the name of the Lord;
praise him, you servants of the LORD,
you who minister in the house of the LORD,
in the courts of the house of our God.

Praise the LORD, for the LORD is good;
sing praise to his name, for that is pleasant.
For the LORD has chosen Jacob to be his own,
Israel to be his treasured possession.

I know that the LORD is great,
that our Lord is greater than all gods.
The LORD does whatever pleases him,
in the heavens and on the earth,
in the seas and all their depths.

Prayer

To your holy name, O Lord, be ascribed honor and glory.

Scripture Reading (Optional)   Hebrews 12:1-12

Intercessions

With adoration and heartfelt devotion to our great and glorious heavenly
Father, let us pray,

Fill our souls entirely with a love of you.

Grant us grace to know you better each day so that the more we know
you, the more we may love you.

Fill our souls entirely with a love of you.

May we always be deeply respectful to you and never use your venerable
name carelessly or in ways that are not worshipful.

Fill our souls entirely with a love of you.

Let it be the one business of our lives to glorify you by our every thought,
word, and deed—even to the point of death, if you call us to it. And may
we engage all people, as far as we are able, to glorify and love you too.

Fill our souls entirely with a love of you.

(Offer personal prayers.)

The Lord's Prayer

Dismissal

O Father, watch over us with your mighty power and grant that this day
we fall into no sin, nor run into any kind of danger, through Jesus Christ
our Lord. Amen.

DAY 23 † Evening Prayer

Self-Examination

(Reflect on the day, using the following questions as a guide, confess any departures from the law of love, and ask God for forgiveness.)

- Have I responded to my neighbor's weaknesses with compassion, not with impatience or anger?
- Have I let my neighbor have the last word in a small matter, even though I thought he or she was wrong?

Opening

O God, come to my assistance; O Lord, make haste to help me (Ps. 69:2, DRA).

Glory to the Father, and to the Son, and to the Holy Spirit: as it was in the beginning, is now, and will be forever. Amen.

Ephesians 1:7-8

In [Christ] we have redemption through his blood, the forgiveness of sins, in accordance with the riches of God's grace that he lavished on us with all wisdom and understanding.

Intercessions

(Offer personal prayers.)

The Lord's Prayer

Dismissal

O Almighty Father, take us this night into your gracious protection and settle our spirits in delightful thoughts of the glory where our Lord Jesus dwells, through whom we pray. Amen.

Personal Meditations

DAY 24 † Morning Prayer

O Lord, open my lips, and my mouth will declare your praise (Ps. 51:15).

Psalm 95:1-2

Come, let us sing for joy to the LORD;
> let us shout aloud to the Rock of our salvation.

Let us come before him with thanksgiving
> and extol him with music and song.

Glory to the Father, and to the Son, and to the Holy Spirit: as it was in the beginning, is now, and will be forever. Amen.

Hymn

God of all redeeming grace,
> *By your pard'ning love compelled,*

Up to you our souls we raise,
> *Up to you our bodies yield.*

Psalm 101:1-3

I will sing of your love and justice;
> to you, O LORD, I will sing praise.

I will be careful to lead a blameless life—
> when will you come to me?

I will walk in my house
> with blameless heart.

I will set before my eyes
> no vile thing.

Prayer

God of all goodness, send down your heavenly grace into our souls so that we can worship and serve you as we ought to do.

Psalm 144:1-2

Praise be to the LORD my Rock,
who trains my hands for war,
my fingers for battle.
He is my loving God and my fortress,
my stronghold and my deliverer,
my shield, in whom I take refuge,
who subdues peoples under me.

Prayer

We praise and bless your name, O Father, for all your mercies and favors and for bringing us safely to the light of a new day.

Scripture Reading (Optional)   Isaiah 55:1-3

Intercessions

With adoration and praise to the gracious Giver of all good things, let us pray,

O Father in heaven, we lift up our hearts to you.

Go before us in all we do today so that in all our thoughts, words, and deeds we may continually glorify your holy name.

O Father in heaven, we lift up our hearts to you.

Grant us the grace to follow in all righteousness and holy living our brothers and sisters in Christ who have gone before us.

O Father in heaven, we lift up our hearts to you.

Let your fatherly hand be ever over us and your Holy Spirit ever with us, and lead us in the knowledge and obedience of your word so that we might obtain everlasting life, through Jesus Christ our Lord.

O Father in heaven, we lift up our hearts to you.

(Offer personal prayers.)

The Lord's Prayer

Dismissal

Most merciful Lord, as you have graciously protected us through the night, so accompany us all this day with your blessing. We ask this through Christ our Redeemer. Amen.

DAY 24 † Evening Prayer

Self-Examination

(Reflect on the day, using the following questions as a guide, confess any departures from the law of love, and ask God for forgiveness.)

- Have I hurt anyone by my word or deed?
- Have I worked hard at my job and been responsible in the use of time?

Opening

O God, come to my assistance; O Lord, make haste to help me (Ps. 69:2, DRA).

Glory to the Father, and to the Son, and to the Holy Spirit: as it was in the beginning, is now, and will be forever. Amen.

Colossians 3:15

Let the peace of Christ rule in your hearts, since as members of one body you were called to peace. And be thankful.

Intercessions

(Offer personal prayers.)

The Lord's Prayer

Dismissal

O Father, now that night has come and we are ready to take our rest, we commit ourselves to your protection, through Jesus Christ our Lord. Amen.

Personal Meditations

DAY 25 † Morning Prayer

O Lord, open my lips, and my mouth will declare your praise (Ps. 51:15).

Psalm 95:6-7

Come, let us bow down in worship,
    let us kneel before the LORD our Maker;
for he is our God
    and we are the people of his pasture,
    the flock under his care.

Glory to the Father, and to the Son, and to the Holy Spirit: as it was in the beginning, is now, and will be forever. Amen.

Hymn

Rejoice, the Lord is King;
    Your Lord and King adore!
Rejoice, give thanks, and sing,
    And triumph evermore.

Psalm 108:1-5

My heart is steadfast, O God;
    I will sing and make music with all my soul.
Awake, harp and lyre!
    I will awaken the dawn.
I will praise you, O LORD, among the nations;
    I will sing of you among the peoples.
For great is your love, higher than the heavens;
    your faithfulness reaches to the skies.
Be exalted, O God, above the heavens,
    and let your glory be over all the earth.

Prayer

O Lord God, we bow and offer to you our praise and thanksgivings for all your mercies to us throughout the night past.

Psalm 146:1-4

Praise the LORD.

Praise the LORD, O my soul.

    I will praise the LORD all my life;

    I will sing praise to my God as long as I live.

Do not put your trust in princes,

    in mortal men, who cannot save.

When their spirit departs, they return to the ground;

    on that very day their plans come to nothing.

Prayer

We bless you, O Father, and entrust ourselves to you, for you alone sustain us when we sleep and when we rise.

Scripture Reading (Optional)   Deuteronomy 4:39-40

Intercessions

To our merciful Father, who has loved us with a marvelous love, let us pray,

    Keep us faithful to the purposes inspired by your Spirit.

Strengthen us with your grace so that we may bring forth all the fruits of righteousness.

    Keep us faithful to the purposes inspired by your Spirit.

Let the goodness of your commands render us fruitful and abundant in your work.

    Keep us faithful to the purposes inspired by your Spirit.

Let all our actions be spirited with zeal, all our zeal regulated with wisdom, and our wisdom joined with perfect integrity of heart.

    Keep us faithful to the purposes inspired by your Spirit.

    (Offer personal prayers.)

The Lord's Prayer

Dismissal

O gracious Father, keep us today from all things hurtful and lead us to all things useful, through Jesus Christ our Savior. Amen.

DAY 25 † Evening Prayer

Self-Examination

(Reflect on the day, using the following questions as a guide, confess any departures from the law of love, and ask God for forgiveness.)
- Have I been charitable in my words to and about others?
- Have I allowed my devout thoughts and feelings to be put into practice in loving service to God and neighbor?

Opening

O God, come to my assistance; O Lord, make haste to help me (Ps. 69:2, DRA).

Glory to the Father, and to the Son, and to the Holy Spirit: as it was in the beginning, is now, and will be forever. Amen.

Colossians 1:18

[Christ] is the head of the body, the church; he is the beginning and the firstborn from among the dead, so that in everything he might have the supremacy.

Intercessions

(Offer personal prayers.)

The Lord's Prayer

Dismissal

O Father, bless us this night and always with the blessings of your children, through Jesus Christ our loving Redeemer. Amen.

Personal Meditations

DAY 26 † Morning Prayer

O Lord, open my lips, and my mouth will declare your praise (Ps. 51:15).

Psalm 24:1-2

The earth is the LORD's, and everything in it,
>   the world, and all who live in it;
> for he founded it upon the seas
>   and established it upon the waters.

Glory to the Father, and to the Son, and to the Holy Spirit: as it was in the beginning, is now, and will be forever. Amen.

Hymn

Jesus, Lover of my soul,
>   *Let me to your bosom fly,*
> *While the nearer waters roll,*
>   *While the tempest still is high!*

Psalm 143:7-10

Answer me quickly, O LORD;
>   my spirit fails.
> Do not hide your face from me
>   or I will be like those who go down to the pit.
> Let the morning bring me word of your unfailing love,
>   for I have put my trust in you.
> Show me the way I should go,
>   for to you I lift up my soul.
> Rescue me from my enemies, O LORD,
>   for I hide myself in you.
> Teach me to do your will,
>   for you are my God;
> may your good Spirit
>   lead me on level ground.

Prayer

O our God, do not withdraw your mercy from us, but let your loving-kindness and truth always preserve us.

Psalm 147:1-3

Praise the LORD.
How good it is to sing praises to our God,
    how pleasant and fitting to praise him!

The LORD builds up Jerusalem;
    he gathers the exiles of Israel.
He heals the brokenhearted
    and binds up their wounds.

Prayer

O Lord, open our eyes to see the wonderful things your love has done.

Scripture Reading (Optional)   Romans 8:18-21

Intercessions

To the God of our salvation, on whom we rest all our hopes, let us pray,
    Guide us, O Lord, and comfort us with your presence.
Watch over us and renew our lives and your mercies.
    Guide us, O Lord, and comfort us with your presence.
Defend us from all our sins and make us zealous in doing good works.
    Guide us, O Lord, and comfort us with your presence.
Sanctify all our activities, our crosses, our comforts, and all the events
that befall us.
    Guide us, O Lord, and comfort us with your presence.

(Offer personal prayers.)

The Lord's Prayer

Dismissal

O eternal Father, incline our ears to wisdom and our hearts to understanding that we may increase in our knowledge and love of you, through Christ our Lord. Amen.

DAY 26 † Evening Prayer

Self-Examination
(Reflect on the day, using the following questions as a guide, confess any departures from the law of love, and ask God for forgiveness.)

- Have I done all I can to keep my mind and body fit for God's service?
- Have I been diligent in my prayers and actions for the salvation of those nearest me who do not know God?

Opening
O God, come to my assistance; O Lord, make haste to help me (Ps. 69:2, DRA).

Glory to the Father, and to the Son, and to the Holy Spirit: as it was in the beginning, is now, and will be forever. Amen.

Colossians 1:21-23
Once you were alienated from God and were enemies in your minds because of your evil behavior. But now he has reconciled you by Christ's physical body through death to present you holy in his sight, without blemish and free from accusation—if you continue in your faith, established and firm, not moved from the hope held out in the gospel.

Intercessions
(Offer personal prayers.)

The Lord's Prayer

Dismissal
O Father, as we take our evening rest, imprint and preserve upon our hearts a lively sense of all your kindness to us, through Jesus Christ our Savior. Amen.

Personal Meditations

DAY 27 † Morning Prayer

O Lord, open my lips, and my mouth will declare your praise (Ps. 51:15).

Psalm 67:1-2

May God be gracious to us and bless us
    and make his face shine upon us,
            Selah
that your ways may be known on earth,
    your salvation among all nations.

Glory to the Father, and to the Son, and to the Holy Spirit: as it was in the beginning, is now, and will be forever. Amen.

Hymn

O give me, Lord, the tender heart
    That trembles at the approach of sin.
A godly fear of sin impart,
    Implant, and root it deep within.

Psalm 51:14-17

Save me from bloodguilt, O God,
    the God who saves me,
    and my tongue will sing of your righteousness.
O Lord, open my lips,
    and my mouth will declare your praise.
You do not delight in sacrifice, or I would bring it;
    you do not take pleasure in burnt offerings.
The sacrifices of God are a broken spirit;
    a broken and contrite heart,
    O God, you will not despise.

Prayer

Enable us, O Lord, to walk before you in holiness and righteousness to your praise and glory.

Psalm 147:7-11

Sing to the LORD with thanksgiving;
>make music to our God on the harp.

He covers the sky with clouds;
>he supplies the earth with rain
>and makes grass grow on the hills.

He provides food for the cattle
>and for the young ravens when they call.

His pleasure is not in the strength of the horse,
>nor his delight in the legs of a man;

the LORD delights in those who fear him,
>who put their hope in his unfailing love.

Prayer

O blessed God, let your mercy and goodness follow us all our lives.

Scripture Reading (Optional)   Galatians 2:16, 19-20

Intercessions

To our God, who searches our hearts and frees us from every weight of sin, let us pray,

>*Speak peace into our souls and keep our hearts turned to you.*

Help us to sense, feel sorrow for, and forsake all our sins.

>*Speak peace into our souls and keep our hearts turned to you.*

Let us never be without the comforting assurance of your forgiveness, your acceptance of us, and your love to us.

>*Speak peace into our souls and keep our hearts turned to you.*

As you take pleasure in the well-being of your servants, so let us take pleasure in serving you.

>*Speak peace into our souls and keep our hearts turned to you.*

>*(Offer personal prayers.)*

The Lord's Prayer

Dismissal

O Father, fill our hearts this day with your love and with all peace and joy in the Holy Spirit, through Christ Jesus. Amen.

DAY 27 † Evening Prayer

Self-Examination

(Reflect on the day, using the following questions as a guide, confess any departures from the law of love, and ask God for forgiveness.)

- Have I forgiven others as I have been forgiven?
- Have I regularly prayed God to strengthen in me those virtues I am weak in?

Opening

O God, come to my assistance; O Lord, make haste to help me (Ps. 69:2, DRA).

Glory to the Father, and to the Son, and to the Holy Spirit: as it was in the beginning, is now, and will be forever. Amen.

Romans 8:1

There is now no condemnation for those who are in Christ Jesus, because through Christ Jesus the law of the Spirit of life set me free from the law of sin and death.

Intercessions

(Offer personal prayers.)

The Lord's Prayer

Dismissal

Now, O God, as we lay down and take our rest this night, we ask you to grant us peace and safety, through your Son, Jesus Christ our Lord. Amen.

Personal Meditations

DAY 28 † Morning Prayer

O Lord, open my lips, and my mouth will declare your praise (Ps. 51:15).

Psalm 67:3-4

May the peoples praise you, O God;
    may all the peoples praise you.
May the nations be glad and sing for joy,
    for you rule the peoples justly
    and guide the nations of the earth.

Glory to the Father, and to the Son, and to the Holy Spirit: as it was in the beginning, is now, and will be forever. Amen.

Hymn

My dying Savior and my God,
    Fountain for guilt and sin,
Sprinkle me ever with your blood,
    And cleanse and keep me clean.

Psalm 92:12-15

The righteous will flourish like a palm tree,
    they will grow like a cedar of Lebanon;
planted in the house of the LORD,
    they will flourish in the courts of our God.
They will still bear fruit in old age,
    they will stay fresh and green,
proclaiming, "The LORD is upright;
    he is my Rock, and there is no wickedness in him."

Prayer

For all your mercies, O God, we bless you, adore your power, and magnify your goodness.

Psalm 113:2-6

Let the name of the LORD be praised,
    both now and forevermore.

From the rising of the sun to the place where it sets,
the name of the LORD is to be praised.
The LORD is exalted over all the nations,
his glory above the heavens.
Who is like the LORD our God,
the One who sits enthroned on high,
who stoops down to look
on the heavens and the earth?

Prayer

Though we are on the earth, O King of heaven, we will praise you and give thanks to you forever and ever.

Scripture Reading (Optional)   2 Peter 3:13-15

Intercessions

With adoration and wholehearted devotion to our gracious and loving Father, let us pray,

May your Holy Spirit renew and sanctify our souls.

In the great name of Christ, we ask for your pardon and peace, the increase of your grace, and the expressions of your love.

May your Holy Spirit renew and sanctify our souls.

Cleanse us from all our sins with the precious blood of Christ, and let all our ways be pleasing in your sight.

May your Holy Spirit renew and sanctify our souls.

O teach us to know you and Jesus Christ whom you have sent, and enable us to do your will on earth, as it is done in heaven.

May your Holy Spirit renew and sanctify our souls.

(Offer personal prayers.)

The Lord's Prayer

Dismissal

Give us grace, O Father, to keep your holy will and commandments today and all the days of our lives, through Christ Jesus, our Lord and Redeemer. Amen.

DAY 28 † Evening Prayer

Self-Examination

(Reflect on the day, using the following questions as a guide, confess any departures from the law of love, and ask God for forgiveness.)

- Have I become too attached to anything in this world so that I have given it a greater priority than my devotion to God?
- Have I been diligent in praying for and serving those suffering from illness, loss, heartache, and loneliness?

Opening

O God, come to my assistance; O Lord, make haste to help me (Ps. 69:2, DRA).

Glory to the Father, and to the Son, and to the Holy Spirit: as it was in the beginning, is now, and will be forever. Amen.

Philippians 2:10-11

At the name of Jesus every knee should bow,
in heaven and on earth and under the earth,
and every tongue confess that Jesus Christ is Lord,
to the glory of God the Father.

Intercessions

(Offer personal prayers.)

The Lord's Prayer

Dismissal

O merciful Father, let us rest in peace this night and not sleep in sin, and grant that we may rise more fit for your service, through Jesus Christ our Lord. Amen.

Personal Meditations

DAY 29 † Morning Prayer

O Lord, open my lips, and my mouth will declare your praise (Ps. 51:15).

Psalm 67:5-7

May the peoples praise you, O God;
    may all the peoples praise you.
Then the land will yield its harvest,
    and God, our God, will bless us.
God will bless us,
    and all the ends of the earth will fear him.

Glory to the Father, and to the Son, and to the Holy Spirit: as it was in the beginning, is now, and will be forever. Amen.

Hymn

Jesus, the Savior, reigns,
    The God of truth and love,
When he had purged our stains,
    He took his seat above.

Psalm 104:1-4

Praise the LORD, O my soul.
O LORD my God, you are very great;
    you are clothed with splendor and majesty.
He wraps himself in light as with a garment;
    he stretches out the heavens like a tent
    and lays the beams of his upper chambers on their waters.
He makes the clouds his chariot
    and rides on the wings of the wind.
He makes winds his messengers,
    flames of fire his servants.

Prayer

O God, may your glorious name be honored and loved by all the creatures you have made.

Psalm 18:1-3

I love you, O LORD, my strength.

The LORD is my rock, my fortress and my deliverer;

> my God is my rock, in whom I take refuge.

> He is my shield and the horn of my salvation, my stronghold.

I call to the LORD, who is worthy of praise,

> and I am saved from my enemies.

Prayer

We rejoice above all things, O Father, that we are in your hands.

Scripture Reading (Optional)   1 Peter 1:3-9

Intercessions

To our merciful God who graciously saves us and guides us, let us pray,

> *Open our understanding to receive your truth.*

Set your truth powerfully upon our hearts and root it deeply in our souls.

> *Open our understanding to receive your truth.*

Let us always so hear, read, mark, learn, and inwardly digest your Word that it may be a savor of life to us.

> *Open our understanding to receive your truth.*

Bless our use of your Word and all the means of grace for the instruction of our minds, the reformation of our lives, and the salvation of our souls.

> *Open our understanding to receive your truth.*

> *(Offer personal prayers.)*

The Lord's Prayer

Dismissal

O Lord, hear our prayers, watch over us, and shine your face upon us throughout this day, for Jesus Christ's sake. Amen.

DAY 29 † Evening Prayer

Self-Examination

(Reflect on the day, using the following questions as a guide, confess any departures from the law of love, and ask God for forgiveness.)

- Have I said or done anything solely to gain the praise of other people?
- Have I despised the advice of anyone?

Opening

O God, come to my assistance; O Lord, make haste to help me (Ps. 69:2, DRA).

Glory to the Father, and to the Son, and to the Holy Spirit: as it was in the beginning, is now, and will be forever. Amen.

2 Corinthians 1:3-4

Praise be to the God and Father of our Lord Jesus Christ, the Father of compassion and the God of all comfort, who comforts us in all our troubles, so that we can comfort those in any trouble with the comfort we ourselves have received from God.

Intercessions

(Offer personal prayers.)

The Lord's Prayer

Dismissal

O Father, let us lay down and sleep in your arms, knowing that your loving care will be with us this night and in the nights and days to come, through Christ Jesus our Lord. Amen.

Personal Meditations

DAY 30 † Morning Prayer

O Lord, open my lips, and my mouth will declare your praise (Ps. 51:15).

Psalm 24:3-5

Who may ascend the hill of the LORD?
> Who may stand in his holy place?
He who has clean hands and a pure heart,
> who does not lift up his soul to an idol
> or swear by what is false.
He will receive blessing from the LORD
> and vindication from God his Savior.

Glory to the Father, and to the Son, and to the Holy Spirit: as it was in the beginning, is now, and will be forever. Amen.

Hymn

Hail! holy, holy, holy Lord!
> *Whom One in Three we know;*
By all your heav'nly host adored,
> *By all your church below.*

Psalm 136:1-3

Give thanks to the LORD, for he is good.
> *His love endures forever.*
Give thanks to the God of gods.
> *His love endures forever.*
Give thanks to the Lord of lords:
> *His love endures forever.*

Prayer

We bless you, O Lord, for all the blessings of this life.

Psalm 34:1-5

I will extol the LORD at all times;
> his praise will always be on my lips.

My soul will boast in the LORD;
    let the afflicted hear and rejoice.
Glorify the LORD with me;
    let us exalt his name together.
I sought the LORD, and he answered me;
    he delivered me from all my fears.
Those who look to him are radiant;
    their faces are never covered with shame.

Prayer

We praise you, O merciful Father, for having granted us pardon and peace.

Scripture Reading (Optional)   1 Thessalonians 5:23-24

Intercessions

With hearts filled with gratitude and adoration to our almighty God and Father, in whom we live and move and have our being, let us pray,

    Praise to you, O Lord, for all your gracious gifts.

You grant us health, food, clothing, peace, safety, friends, family, and all the blessings in this life.

    Praise to you, O Lord, for all your gracious gifts.

You give us a desire to attain life eternal, allowing us to feel in our hearts our yearning for you.

    Praise to you, O Lord, for all your gracious gifts.

We now offer ourselves to you. Inspire us by your love to a greater zeal and devotion in our service to you and all our neighbors.

    Praise to you, O Lord, for all your gracious gifts.

(Offer personal prayers.)

The Lord's Prayer

Dismissal

Keep us, O Father, this day from all things hurtful to our souls and bodies, and grant us a pure heart and mind to follow the steps of our gracious Redeemer, in whose name we pray. Amen.

DAY 30 † Evening Prayer

Self-Examination

(Reflect on the day, using the following questions as a guide, confess any departures from the law of love, and ask God for forgiveness.)

- Have I sought to be cheerful, mild, and courteous in whatever I said or did?
- Have I rejoiced or grieved with my neighbor?
- Have I zealously done what good I could?

Opening

O God, come to my assistance; O Lord, make haste to help me (Ps. 69:2, DRA).

Glory to the Father, and to the Son, and to the Holy Spirit: as it was in the beginning, is now, and will be forever. Amen.

1 John 3:1

How great is the love the Father has lavished on us, that we should be called children of God! And that is what we are!

Intercessions

(Offer personal prayers.)

The Lord's Prayer

Dismissal

O Lord, let us fall asleep with holy thoughts of you, and when we awake, let us be still present with you, through Jesus Christ our Savior. Amen.

Personal Meditations

Sources

The prayers and hymns used in this book were adapted from the following sources:

Bible, Ken, comp. *Wesley Hymns*. Kansas City: Lillenas Publishing Co., 1982. Lyrics used are by Charles Wesley, except for Gerhard Tersteegen, "Lo, God Is Here! Let Us Adore" (day 15), and Joachim Lange, "O God, What Offering Shall I Give?" (day 16), which were translated by John Wesley from the German.

Book of Common Prayer. New York: Church Hymnal Corporation, 1979.

Wesley, John. "A Collection of Forms of Prayer, for Every Day in the Week." In *The Works of John Wesley*. 3rd ed. Edited by Thomas Jackson. 1872. Reprint, Kansas City: Beacon Hill Press of Kansas City, 1986, 11:203-37.

———. "A Collection of Prayers for Families." In Jackson, *Works of John Wesley*, 11:237-59.

———. "Prayers for Children." In Jackson, *Works of John Wesley*, 11:259-72.

———. "A Scheme of Self-Examination." In Jackson, *Works of John Wesley*, 11:521-23.

Most of the Scripture selections follow the order of the four-week prayer cycle of the Latin breviary. Several websites contain English translations of this ancient source, including http://www.universalis.com and http://www.liturgies.net/Liturgies/Catholic/loh/loh.htm.